COVER AND INTERIOR ILLUSTRATIONS BY
SIRREESE AND A. CLARKE
TEXT BY A. CLARKE.

MEET THE RENAISSANCE FEMALES

LONDONN

LONDONN

LONDONN

LONDONN

LONDONN

LONDONN

<table>
<tr><td>Monday</td><td>Tuesday</td><td>Wednesday</td><td>Thursday</td><td>Friday</td><td>Saturday</td><td>Sunday</td></tr>
</table>

Plan The Best Week Of Your Life

9

10

11

12

13

14

15

16

17

18

19

20

Done

RENAISSANCE FEMALES

PARISS

LONDONN

Milann

Angelees

WWW.SIRREESE.COM

RENAISSANCE FEMALES

PARISS

LONDONN

Milann

Angelees

I AM SPECIAL

You decide who you are and what you are good at...fill in the list

I AM clever

I AM good at what i do

I AM ......

I ....

RENAISSANCE FEMALES

I CAN ...

I WILL ...

I LIKE ....

I AM ...

PARISS
LONDONN
Milann
Angelees

LONDONN

LONDONN

LONDONN

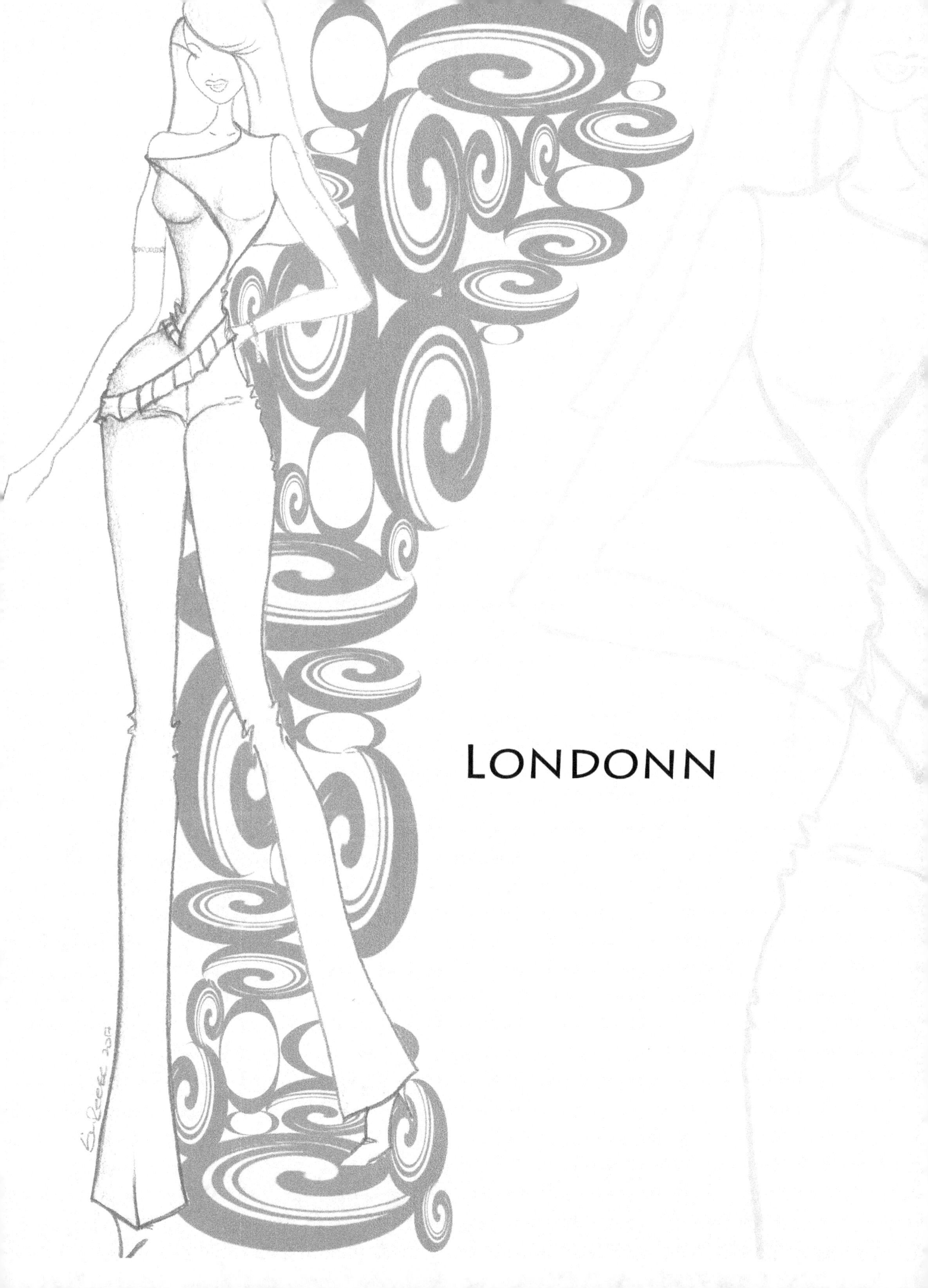

LONDONN

LONDONN

LONDONN

SIR REESE®
WWW.SIRREESE.COM